ULTIMATE STICKER COLLECTION

How to use this book

•

Read the captions, then find the sticker that best fits the space. (Hint: check the sticker labels for clues!)

•

There are lots of fantastic extra stickers for creating your own scenes.

DK Penguin Random House

Written by Julia March
Edited by Ruth Amos
Designed by Thelma-Jane Robb

First published in Great Britain in 2021 by Dorling Kindersley Limited
One Embassy Gardens, 8 Viaduct Gardens, London SW11 7BW
A Penguin Random House Company

10 9 8 7 6 5 4 3 2
004–321866–May/2021

The authorised representative in the EEA is Dorling Kindersley Verlag GmbH. Arnulfstr. 124, 80636 Munich, Germany.

A CIP catalogue record for this book is available from the British Library.

ISBN: 978-0-24146-931-6

Printed in China

For the curious
www.dk.com
www.LEGO.com

MIX Paper from responsible sources FSC™ C018179

This book was made with Forest Stewardship Council ™ certified paper – one small step in DK's commitment to a sustainable future. For more information go to www.dk.com/our-green-pledge

WELCOME TO JURASSIC WORLD!

A visit to Jurassic World is a dinosaur lover's dream. This amazing theme park has balloon trips, monorails, and museums. It has cafés, stalls, and gift shops. And it has what every visitor wants to see most – living, breathing, roaring, chomping dinosaurs!

RIDE ENTRANCE

A sign over this entrance gate shows visitors which ride they are about to experience. It's the Egg Spinner ride!

SIGNPOST

Which way to the Gyrosphere ride? Where is the gift shop? Visitors need only look for a signpost to find out.

LUSH LOCATION

Jurassic World is built on Isla Nublar, off the coast of Central America. This lush island is covered in jungles, mountains, and waterfalls.

CLAIRE DEARING

Claire is the director of park operations. She makes sure every visitor stays safe and every dinosaur stays happy and healthy.

OWEN GRADY

Owen is the *Velociraptor* trainer. It's a tiring job. *Velociraptors* – *Raptors* for short – are lively, clever, and curious dinosaurs!

MINI LABORATORY

This laboratory contains an incubator where dinosaur eggs are hatched. It keeps them at the ideal temperature.

MARKET STALL

Everything is dinosaur themed in Jurassic World. This market stall looks as if it is clamped in the jaws of a giant carnivore.

HUNGRY VISITOR

Meat eater, plant eater, or ice cream eater? Visitors can buy a variety of treats at the park's food stalls.

JURASSIC WORLD STAFF

A large team of staff keeps Jurassic World running smoothly. Everybody does their bit, from park owner Simon Masrani to the workers who clean the pens. Dinos can be dangerous, so staff must trust each other and try to work together. It's not always easy!

DR HENRY WU

Dr Wu creates the park's dinosaurs in his laboratory. He is very ambitious and likes to make new scientific breakthroughs.

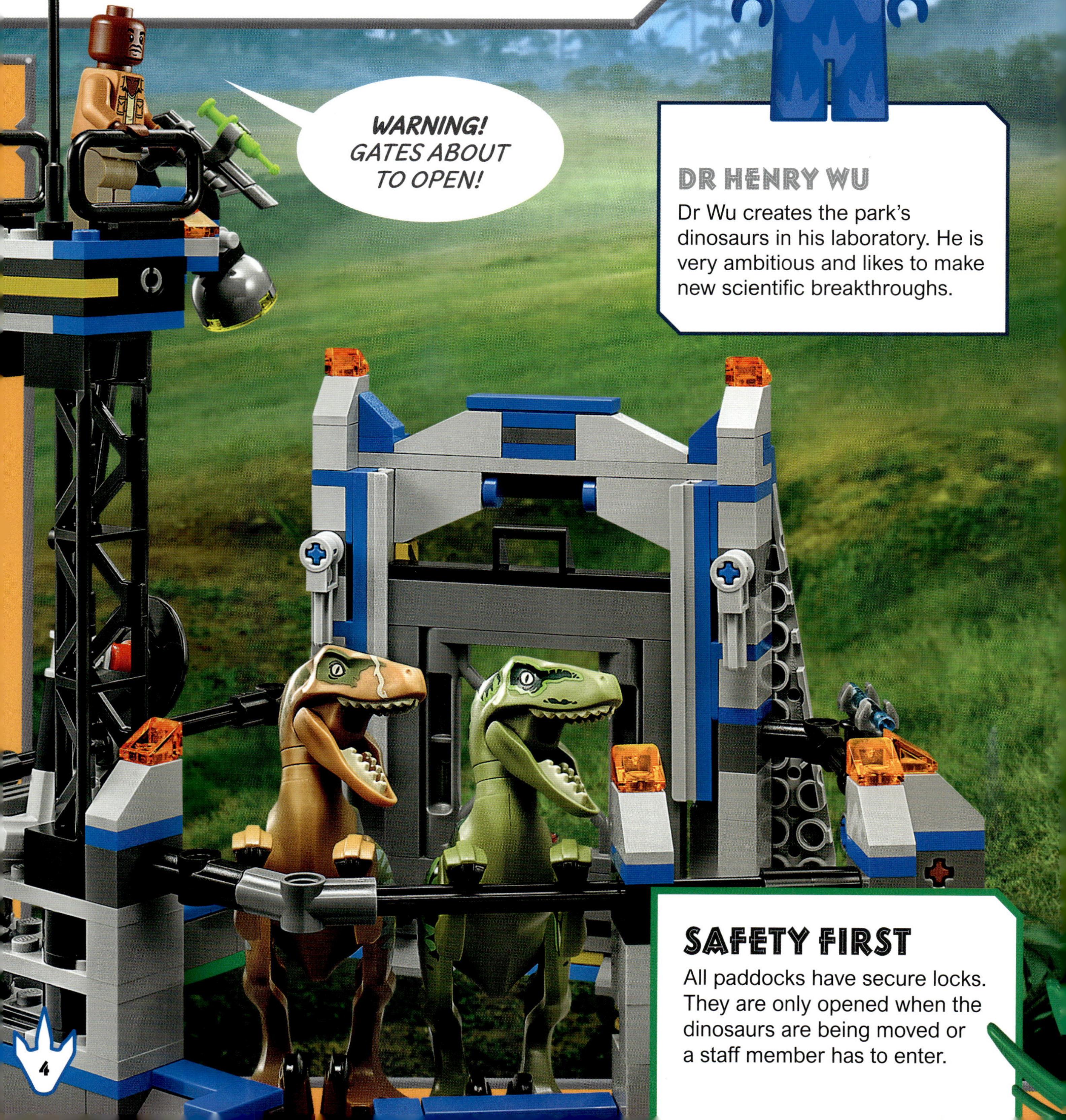

SAFETY FIRST

All paddocks have secure locks. They are only opened when the dinosaurs are being moved or a staff member has to enter.

DR ALLISON MILES

Dr Miles is a scientist who works closely with Dr Wu. She is super-clever and is great at coming up with new ideas.

PARK WORKER

It takes a lot of sweeping to clean out a dino pen. Staff just have to hold their noses and get on with this unpleasant task!

SIMON MASRANI

Simon is the big boss, so he has final say in how the park is run. This optimistic guy is never quite prepared when things go wrong.

ACU TROOPER

If a dino escapes, this ACU (Asset Containment Unit) Trooper must search for her, tranquillisers in hand.

DINOSAUR DOCTOR

A palaeoveterinarian needs nerves of steel. Imagine setting a 3-metre (10-foot) leg bone or stitching a cut on a *T. rex*'s nose!

A FUN TIME FOR ALL

There are so many fun things to do at Jurassic World, it's no wonder visitors get excited. But whether they are whirling on a thrilling ride or seeing dinosaurs up close, all visitors must obey the safety rules. Everyone wants to go home with only happy memories.

ZACH MITCHELL

Zach is Claire's 16-year-old nephew. He thinks he is too cool for rules, so he drives his Gyrosphere into a dangerous restricted area. Not so cool!

GRAY MITCHELL

Zach's little brother is called Gray. Gray is so excited to be at Jurassic World, he can't stop talking. Zach finds that very, very uncool.

EGG SPINNER

On the Egg Spinner, visitors are whirled around in cars shaped like dinosaur eggs. This ride is also called the Scrambler.

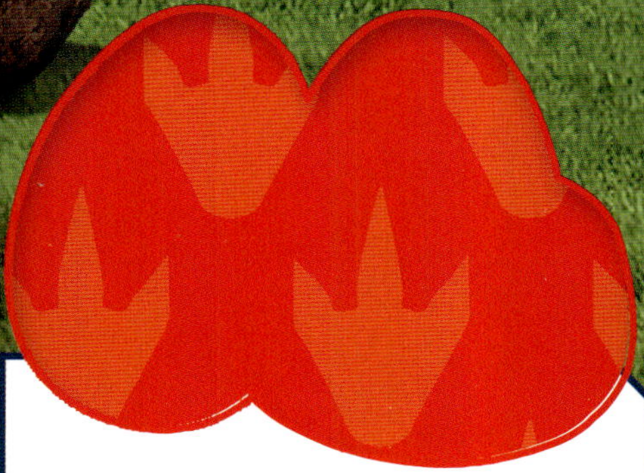

THE HATCHERY

Visitors can peek into the laboratory incubators to look at the dinosaur eggs. If they are lucky, they might see one start to hatch.

GYROSPHERE STATION

Everyone wants a ride in a Gyrosphere! These see-through, round vehicles roll among the dinos. It's very exciting, but strict safety rules must be obeyed.

HUDSON HARPER

Young Hudson won't forget his visit. He has bought a bright dinosaur poster from one of the souvenir stands.

GALLIMIMUS

This baby *Gallimimus* can be fed in the Gentle Giants Petting Zoo. Visitors must take off any straw hats before entering so the dinos don't try to eat them!

GYROSPHERES

A Gyrosphere rolls at up to 8 kph (5 mph). That does not seem very fast when a fierce Indominus rex is chasing you, as Zach discovers.

CARNIVORES

Small or large, carnivores have two things in common: they all love meat, and they are all dangerous! It takes a gifted expert such as Owen Grady to train some of these speedy, sharp-toothed predators.

PTERANODONS

These fierce, flying reptiles live in a big glass dome called the Aviary. If they escape, look out below!

DILOPHOSAURUS

Visitors must not get too close to this double-crested *Dilophosaurus*. If she feels threatened, she might spit poison out at them!

HUNGRY T. REX

Watching the *T. rex* gulp down chunks of meat is a popular attraction at Jurassic World. It is feeding time every two hours. *T. rex* is a very hungry dino!

BLUE THE VELOCIRAPTOR

Blue is the smartest of the *Velociraptors*. She has a special bond with Owen and does whatever he asks of her – mostly!

DELTA

Delta has bird DNA and struts like a bird. Owen keeps a close eye on Delta with this camera head harness. It helps him track her movements.

BARYONYX

The *Baryonyx* usually eats fish. However, if she escapes, she might decide to add a little variety to her diet. Gulp!

CARNOTAURUS

Carnotaurus means "meat-eating bull." It is the perfect name for this bulky dino. She has two horns and a huge appetite for meat.

ECHO AND CHARLIE

The other two *Velociraptors* are Echo and Charlie. Charlie is the youngest of the *Raptor* pack and can be unpredictable!

HERBIVORES

Baby plant eaters can be cute, but watch out for the adults! A heavy herbivore on the loose is bad news at Jurassic World. She won't try to eat the visitors, but she may trample anything in her path.

CARROT LURE

A *Triceratops* has escaped – but don't panic. Owen has attached a carrot to his off-roader vehicle. He will soon have the hungry herbivore trotting behind him, right back to her paddock.

WRECKED FENCE

How do you know which way an escaped herbivore has gone? Just follow the trail of squashed plants and wrecked fences!

ON THE RAMPAGE

The *Triceratops* has already done lots of damage to park equipment. Time to call Maintenance!

ANKYLOSAURUS

The *Ankylosaurus* has bony armour all over her body. Her beak-like jaws are perfect for chomping on low-growing plants.

TERRIBLE TAIL

An *Ankylosaurus*'s tail ends in a bony club. When the dino gets upset, she swings it around. A visitor would not want to get in the way of that!

STYGIMOLOCH

Make way for *Stygimoloch*! This long-legged dino runs very fast. If anything gets in her way, she rams it with her bony head.

STYGIMOLOCH'S PADDOCK

The *Stygimoloch*'s paddock is covered in bars, locks, alarms, and warning signs. Better safe than sorry.

Use the extra stickers to create your own scene.

DR WU'S LABORATORY

Simon Masrani likes to give visitors new things to see all the time. It is Dr Wu's job to create ever more exciting dinosaurs. In his lab at Jurassic World, Dr Wu is performing some very risky experiments.

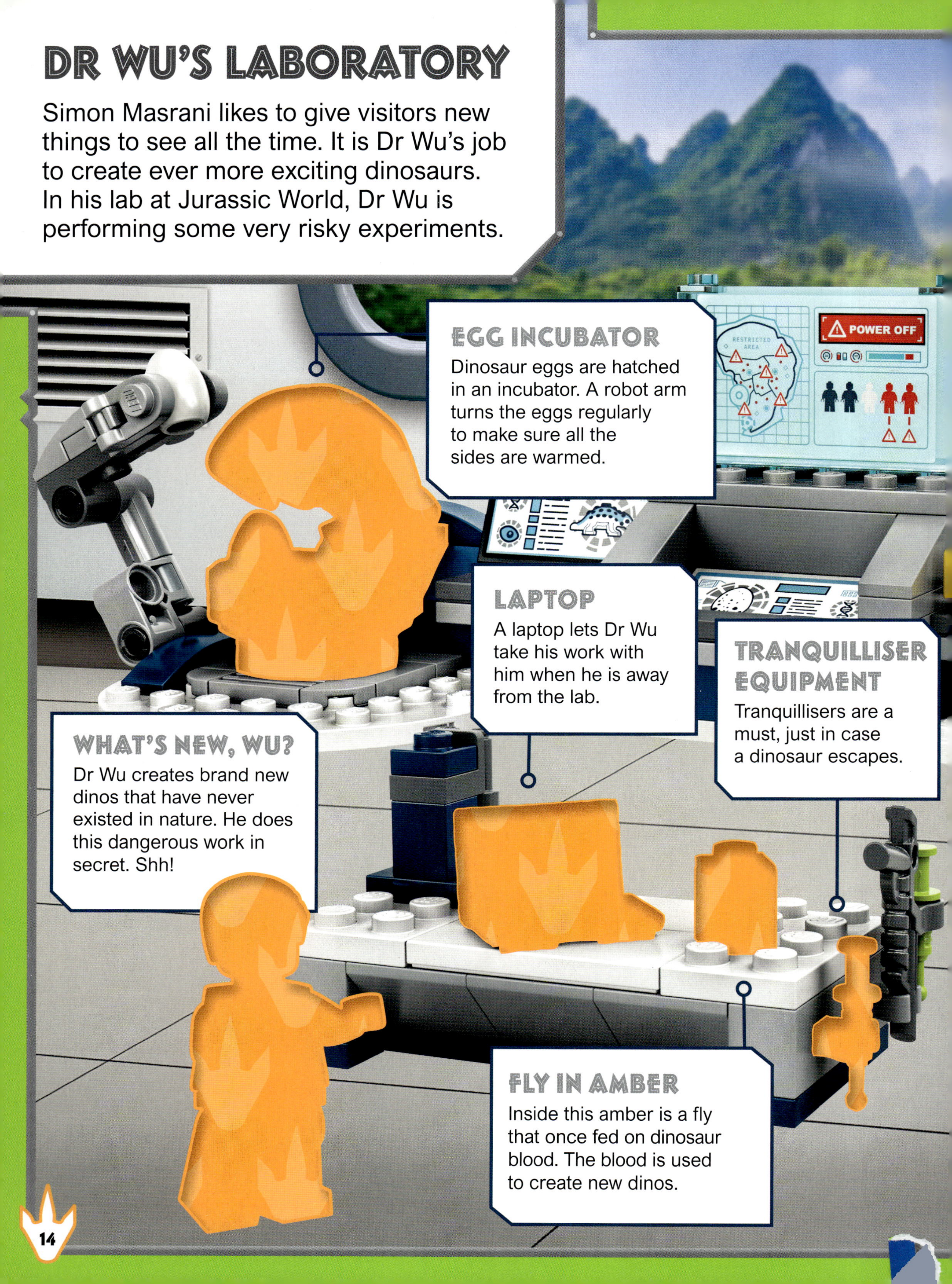

EGG INCUBATOR

Dinosaur eggs are hatched in an incubator. A robot arm turns the eggs regularly to make sure all the sides are warmed.

LAPTOP

A laptop lets Dr Wu take his work with him when he is away from the lab.

TRANQUILLISER EQUIPMENT

Tranquillisers are a must, just in case a dinosaur escapes.

WHAT'S NEW, WU?

Dr Wu creates brand new dinos that have never existed in nature. He does this dangerous work in secret. Shh!

FLY IN AMBER

Inside this amber is a fly that once fed on dinosaur blood. The blood is used to create new dinos.

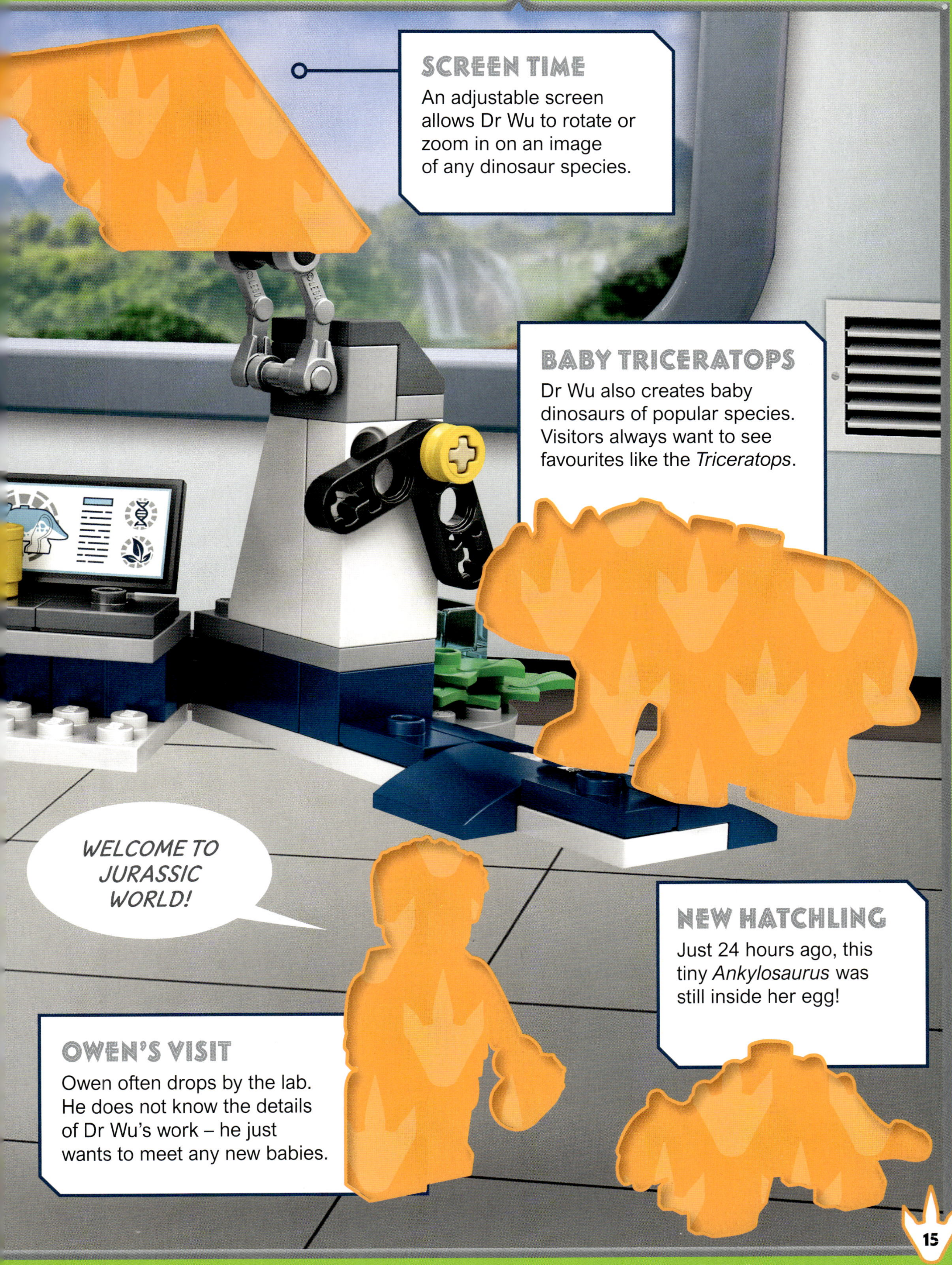

SCREEN TIME

An adjustable screen allows Dr Wu to rotate or zoom in on an image of any dinosaur species.

BABY TRICERATOPS

Dr Wu also creates baby dinosaurs of popular species. Visitors always want to see favourites like the *Triceratops*.

NEW HATCHLING

Just 24 hours ago, this tiny *Ankylosaurus* was still inside her egg!

OWEN'S VISIT

Owen often drops by the lab. He does not know the details of Dr Wu's work – he just wants to meet any new babies.

HYBRID DINOSAURS

A hybrid is a mix of different species. Dr Wu's hybrid dinosaurs are intelligent, fast, and just as exciting as normal dinos. They are called the Indominus rex and the Indoraptor.

PREDATOR'S EYE

Indominus rex's fierce red eyes look a little like a snake's. She does have some modern-day viper in her DNA!

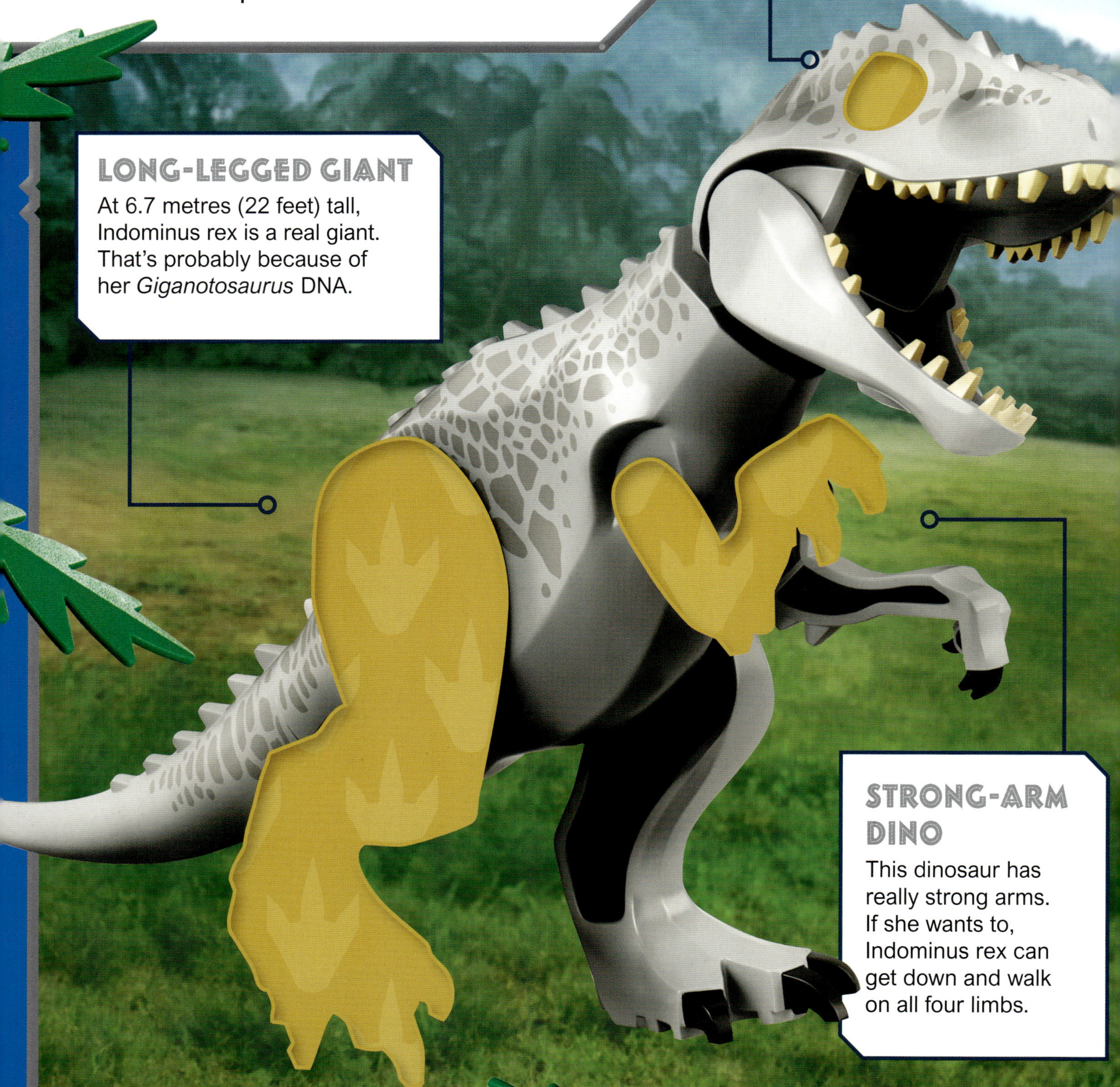

LONG-LEGGED GIANT

At 6.7 metres (22 feet) tall, Indominus rex is a real giant. That's probably because of her *Giganotosaurus* DNA.

STRONG-ARM DINO

This dinosaur has really strong arms. If she wants to, Indominus rex can get down and walk on all four limbs.

SNARLING FACE

The Indoraptor is a hybrid of Indominus rex and *Velociraptor*. He has ragged teeth and reddish eyes that can see in the dark.

STRIPED TAIL

A stripe runs along the Indoraptor's body, right to the end of his tail. He gets this from his *Velociraptor* DNA.

BIG MISTAKE!

Dr Wu tries to make the hybrid dinos trainable, so they will obey commands. He fails!

HUGE CLAWS

The Indoraptor's claws are very long. They are perfect for grabbing prey – or people who get too close.

VILLAINS

Sometimes humans can be as dangerous as dinos! From scheming Jurassic World worker Danny Nedermeyer to thieving adventurer Sinjin Prescott, there always seems to be someone stirring up trouble.

ELI MILLS

Greedy businessman Eli only cares about money. When a volcano is about to erupt on Isla Nublar and destroy the dinos, Eli secretly plots to sell them to the highest bidder.

KEN WHEATLEY

Ken pretends to rescue the dinosaurs from the eruption. In fact, Eli is paying him to steal them! Ken has a cruel hobby – pulling out dinos' teeth for his collection.

VIC HOSKINS

As head of park security, Vic likes zapping things – especially unruly dinos. Arrogant Vic always thinks he knows best!

GUNNAR EVERSOL

Gunnar is the auctioneer who will sell Eli's dinosaurs. He puts profit firmly before safety – until the dinos start chasing him!

MERCENARY

A mercenary will do anything he or she is paid to do. And if this guard is paid well, he is happy to ignore any shady dealings!

TRACKER

This hired guard is in Ken's team of heartless mercenaries. She's a crack shot with her tranquilliser darts.

SINJIN PRESCOTT

Somewhere on Isla Nublar, there is lost treasure! Danny hires this utterly unscrupulous map master to help locate and steal it.

DEVIOUS DANNY

Danny Nedermeyer is not the happy IT guy he seems to be. Alone in an old trailer, Danny plots to sabotage Jurassic World.

BARYONYX FACE-OFF

Bad guys Danny and Sinjin try to find treasure hidden in the jungle. They anger a *Baryonyx* dinosaur and have to take cover in an old trailer! Owen and Claire rush to the scene to stop the thieves.

OLD TRAILER

The old trailer belonged to Danny's uncle, Dennis Nedry. He lived in it years ago, when he was looking for the treasure.

SHADY SIDEKICK

Danny's accomplice, Sinjin, hunts for the treasure. He uses his machete to hack through the dense jungle vegetation.

DANGEROUS DINO

The *Baryonyx* dinosaur thinks that Danny and Sinjin are trying to steal her fish and chases them away.

IMPORTANT CLUE

Sinjin has a treasure map of the island, but part of it is missing. Danny steals an old videotape of Dennis. It shows him with the final piece of the map!

HIDDEN TREASURE

Using the videotape and the rest of the map, Sinjin and Danny find the treasure. This deceitful duo can't stop smiling!

KIND CLAIRE

Claire hopes to find Danny and Sinjin before they get hurt. Even villains don't deserve a battering from a bad-tempered *Baryonyx*!

OWEN AND RED

Owen is a dinosaur behaviour expert, so he knows what to do in a dino emergency. His dog, Red, is often with him.

OFF-ROAD BUGGY

Owen and Claire jump into their buggy to get to the scene quickly. It's the best way to get around the bumpy jungle floor.

Use the extra stickers to create your own scene.

DINOSAUR BREAKOUT!

Emergency! Emergency! A *Gallimimus* and a *Pteranodon* have escaped their enclosures! Can Claire and Owen capture the beasts before they do any damage – or even worse, someone gets hurt?

UNPILOTED DRONE

Owen sends a remote-controlled drone up high over the park to look for the *Pteranodon*. There she is!

DETACHABLE LAB

A mini lab attaches to the back of the research vehicle. Inside is everything an injured dinosaur might need.

RESEARCH VEHICLE

Claire chases down the *Gallimimus* in her research vehicle. Then she fires a net to capture the dino. Got her!

ACU ASSISTANCE

“Dino heading east. Do you copy, Claire?” An ACU Trooper uses a walkie-talkie to assist the dino chasers.

STAYING SAFE

Owen takes a tranquilliser from the back of the vehicle. A sleepy dinosaur is much easier to capture.

GALLIMIMUS CAPTURED!

The runaway *Gallimimus* gives a squawk of defeat as Claire’s net closes. Her hour of freedom is over!

DINOSAUR PROTECTION GROUP

The Dinosaur Protection Group (DPG) is a team of volunteers led by Claire Dearing. They aim to keep dinosaurs safe. Mount Sibo, a long-dormant volcano on Isla Nublar, is about to erupt. The DPG must get the dinos off the burning island and onto evacuation boats. Hurry!

FRANKLIN WEBB

Franklin works on the DPG's technology team. He definitely prefers to be at his computer rather than in the middle of the dangerous action!

ZIA RODRIGUEZ

Zia is the DPG's palaeoveterinarian. She wishes the government would do more to help save the stranded dinos on Isla Nublar.

ROLL AWAY

Franklin escapes a lava pit but then gets chased by a *Carnotaurus*. He flees in a Gyrosphere. Roll, Franklin, roll!

RUN TO THE RESCUE!

Look out – it's going to blow! As the volcano erupts, Claire and Owen run to organise the evacuation of the dinos.

T. REX TRANSFUSION

The *T. rex* has been injured by flying rocks. She needs a blood transfusion. "How many gallons?" wonders Zia.

MEAN MERCENARIES

These mercenaries pretend to help the DPG rescue the dinosaurs. But really, the crooks dino-nap them to be sold at auction by Eli Mills.

ERUPTION!

Red and orange lava streams from the erupting volcano. Some bats that were living in it escape just in time.

TROUBLE AT LOCKWOOD ESTATE

Sir Benjamin Lockwood is one of Jurassic World's founders. This elderly man trusts Eli Mills to run his business, but he really shouldn't. Eli plans to make a fortune by auctioning off the stolen dinos, right in Sir Benjamin's own mansion.

MAISIE

Sir Benjamin's grandaughter, Maisie, uncovers Eli's plan. If only her grandfather would listen to her warning!

LOCKWOOD MANSION

Sir Benjamin's grand mansion is huge. It's easy for evil Eli to hold an event in one part of the building without Sir Benjamin even knowing about it!

BALCONY CLIMB

At the auction, the Indoraptor is accidentally released! To dodge him, Maisie climbs up the building. Claire helps her onto the balcony.

EVIL AUCTIONEERS

"Going, going, gone!" Eli and Gunnar have to get going themselves when the dangerous dinos come after them.

ESCAPED INDORAPTOR

The escaped Indoraptor peers into every room, looking for potential prey. Peekaboo!

OWEN VS KEN

Owen is ready to fight Ken Wheatley. Ken pretended to be his ally, then betrayed him and stole Blue the *Velociraptor* for Eli.

GRRR!

CAGED T. REX

Caged and ready for auction, the *T. rex* roars angrily. Now that Claire and Owen are on the scene, she will soon be free.

TECHNOLOGY FOR TRAVEL

No part of Isla Nublar is out of reach to Jurassic World staff. That's because of the amazing vehicles and gadgets the tech team has created. Wherever a dino can go, these vehicles can go, too – through mud, jungle, water, or even the air.

HELICOPTER

Simon Masrani is flying solo in his helicopter. He plans to catch a stray *Pteranodon* on his own. Is that wise?!

MOBILE VET UNIT

The mobile vet unit has a rooftop shooter for firing tranquilliser darts. Injured dinos can be dangerous until they are sedated.

BOAT AFLOAT

This is a narrow part of the river! Owen uses the rudder to carefully steer the yellow boat while Claire watches out for hazards ahead.

BIPLANE

If a human is cornered by a dinosaur, Owen flies to the rescue in his biplane. He lets down a chain for the human to grab.

ALL-TERRAIN VEHICLE

An ACU Trooper can handle any terrain in this rugged 4x4 vehicle, with its big rubber tyres. The cable winch is useful for tripping up a fleeing dinosaur.

PILOTED DRONE

A drone is much quieter than a helicopter. Owen uses this drone to swoop down and throw a net over an escaped dino.

DINO MECH

That's no dinosaur – it's a dino-shaped fighting machine. But who is that driving it? It's Danny Nedermeyer! He's up to no good, as usual...

OFF-ROADER

Speed, manoeuvrability, power – this compact off-roader has them all. It is *Raptor* trainer Barry Sembène's favourite ride.

BABY DINOSAURS

At Jurassic World, visitors can feed, pet, and even ride some of the cute baby herbivores. Carnivore babies are not safe to pet, but they are fun to watch. Trainer Owen has taught the *Raptors* all kinds of tricks.

VELOCIRAPTOR PLAYPEN

A bored *Velociraptor* is a dangerous *Velociraptor*. It takes a lot of toys to stop these intelligent babies from getting up to mischief.

BABY ANKYLOSAURUS

Baby herbivores get along well. This *Ankylosaurus* happily shares her pen with a *Triceratops*.

TRICERATOPS RIDE

Once she has been trained to wear a saddle, the gentle baby *Triceratops* will be ready to give rides to young visitors.

OWEN'S RAPTOR PACK

Owen began training Blue, Charlie, Echo, and Delta when they were babies. He had to be sensitive but strict.

Claire Dearing

Gallimimus

Dilophosaurus

Tracker

Off-road buggy

Piloted drone

Roll away

Ride entrance

Park worker

Egg incubator

Important clue

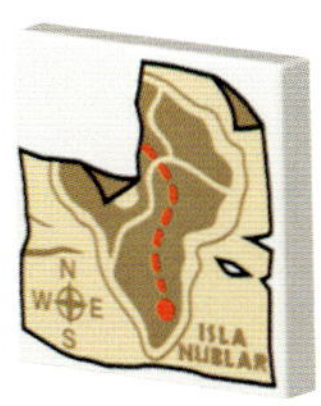

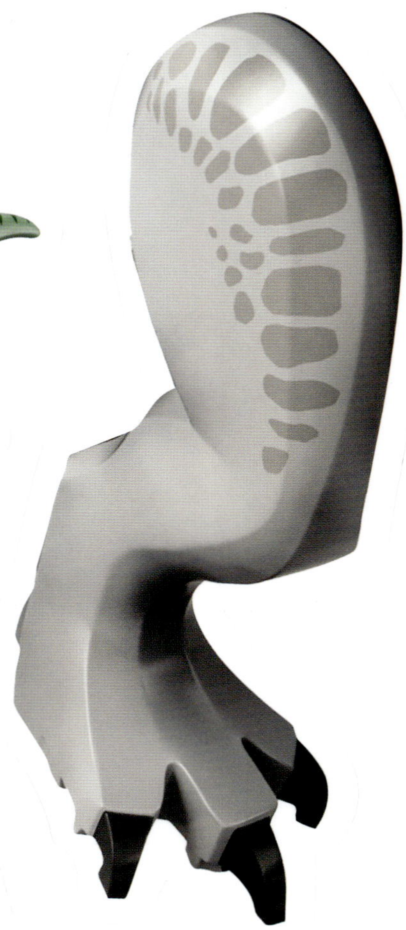

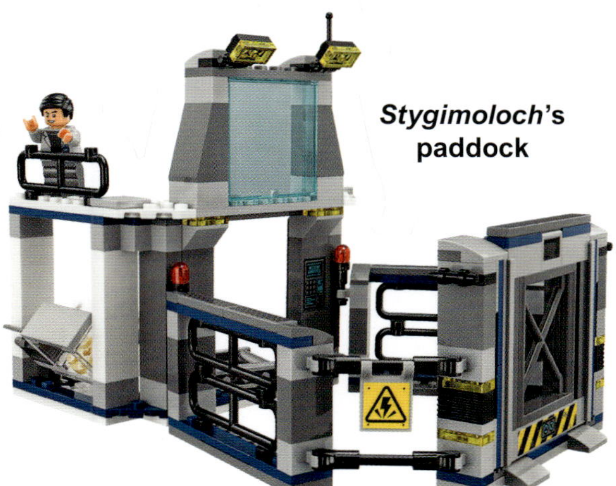

Stygimoloch's paddock

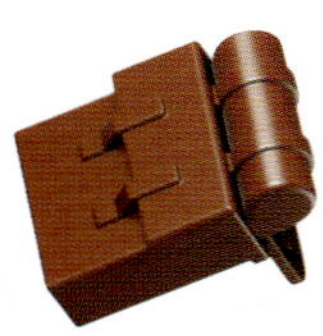

Off-roader

Long-legged giant

Franklin Webb

Gyrosphere station

Pteranodons

What's new, Wu?

Stygimoloch

Ken Wheatley

Predator's eye

All-terrain vehicle

Owen Grady

Dinosaur doctor

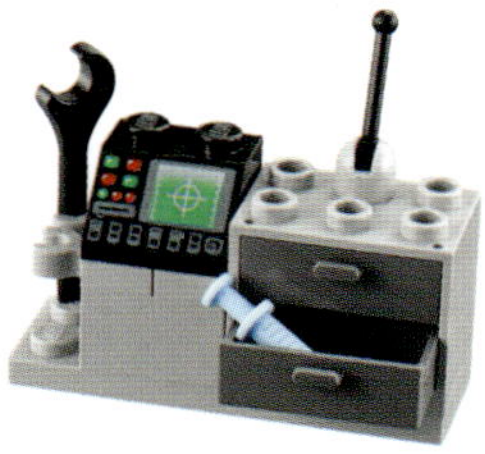

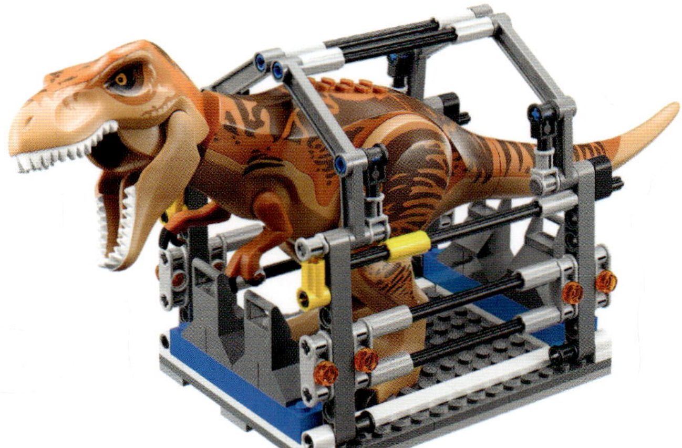

Caged *T. rex*

Market stall

Zia
Rodriguez

Velociraptor playpen

Mobile vet unit

Blue the *Velociraptor*

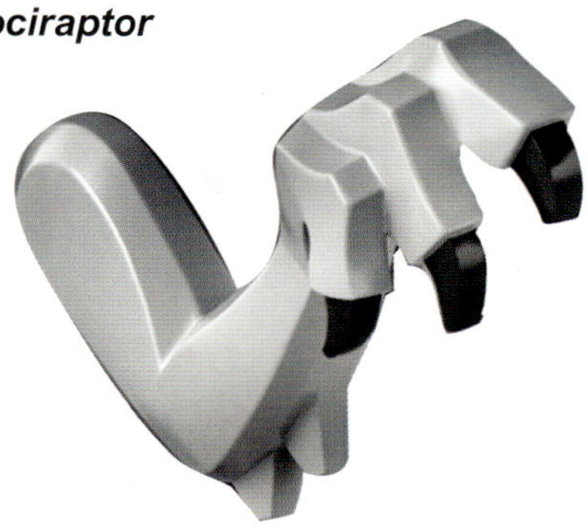

Strong-arm dino

ACU Trooper

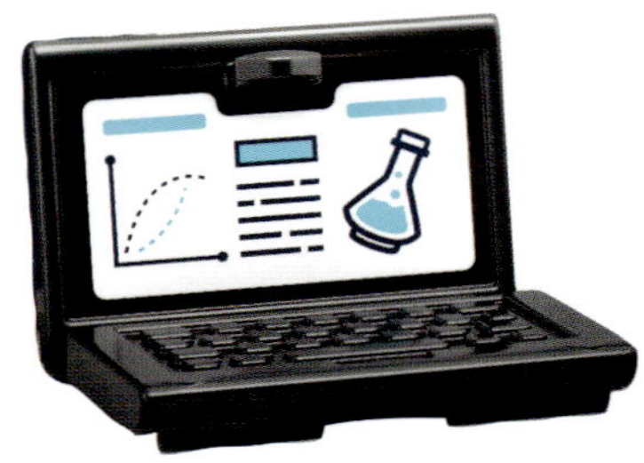

Laptop

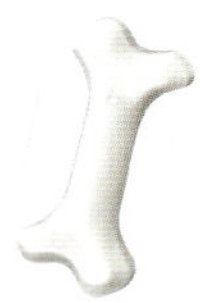

Gunnar Eversol

Old trailer

ACU assistance

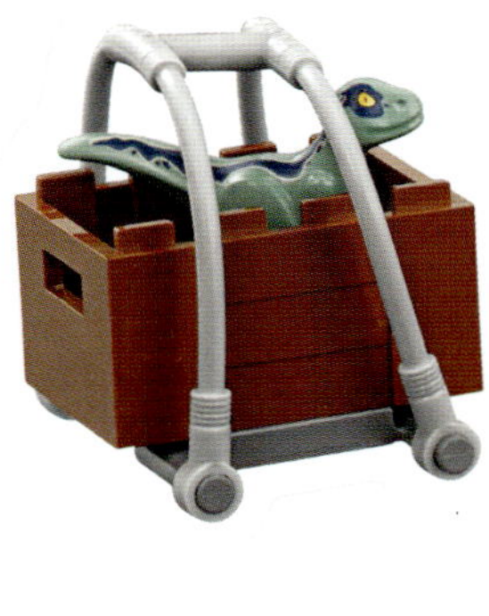

Terrible tail

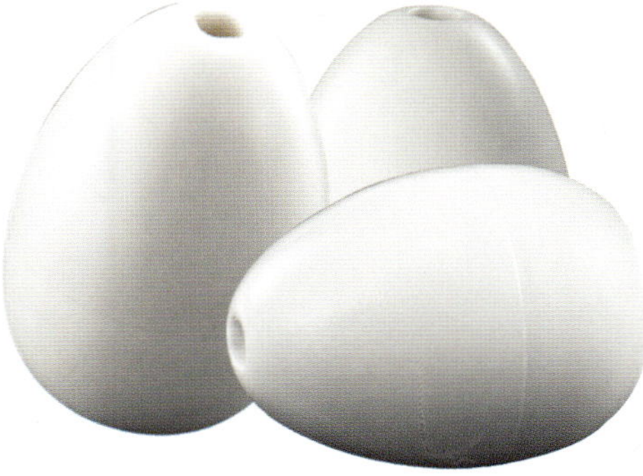

The Hatchery

Owen's *Raptor* pack

Owen and Red

Triceratops ride

New hatchling

Mini laboratory

Hudson Harper

Maisie

Delta

Unpiloted drone

Snarling face

Evil auctioneers

Hidden treasure

Fly in amber

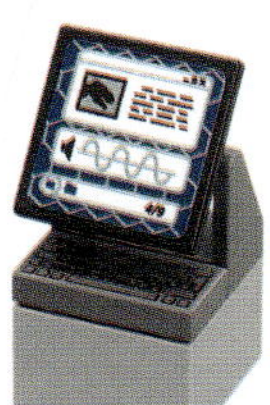

Simon Masrani

Ankylosaurus

Gray Mitchell

Signpost

Dino mech

Balcony climb

Baryonyx

Run to the rescue!

Mercenary

Hungry visitor
Baby *Ankylosaurus*
Wrecked fence
Tranquilliser equipment
Kind Claire
Eli Mills
Shady sidekick
Helicopter
Echo and Charlie

Big mistake!

Baby *Triceratops*

Striped tail

Mean mercenaries

Escaped Indoraptor

Zach Mitchell

T. rex transfusion

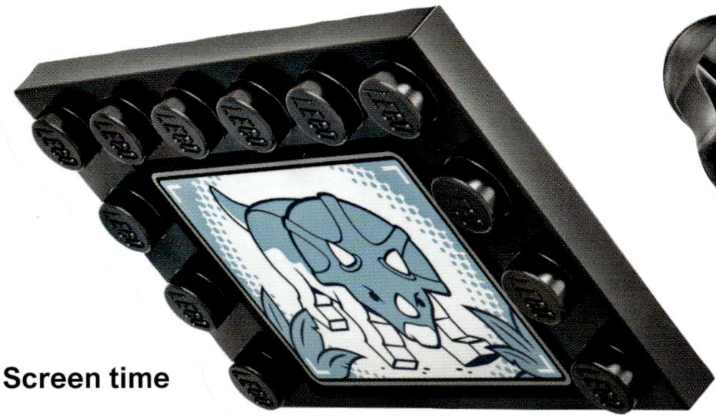

Screen time

Huge claws

Dr Allison Miles

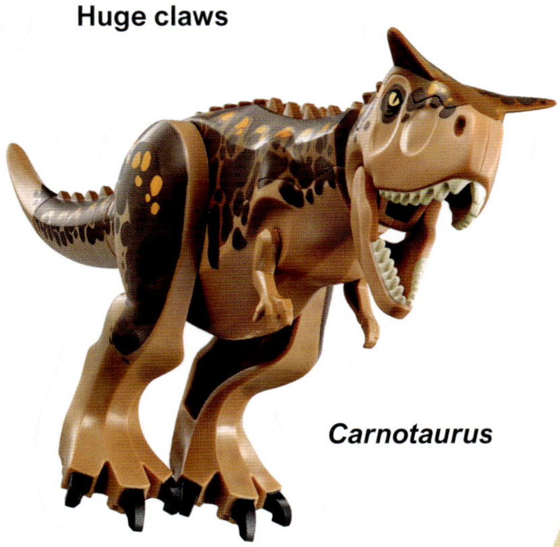

Carnotaurus

Carrot lure

Vic Hoskins

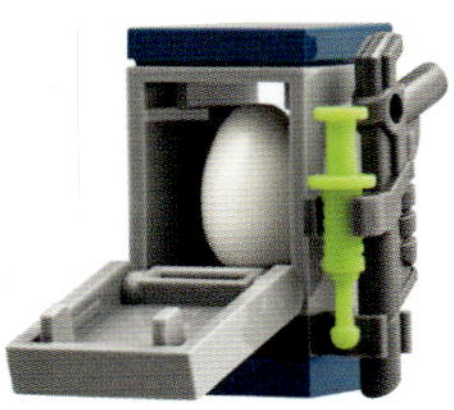

Sinjin Prescott

Egg spinner

Owen vs Ken

Owen's visit

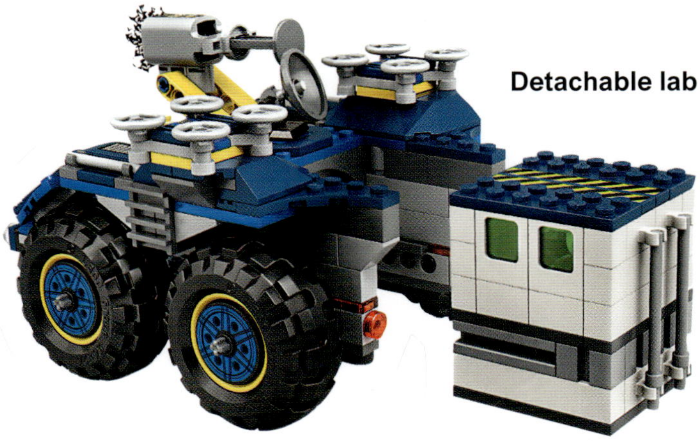

Detachable lab

Gallimimus captured!

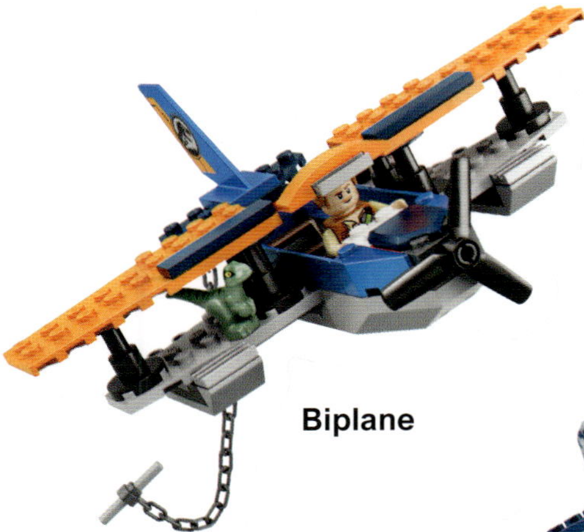

Biplane

Dr Henry Wu

Staying safe

EXTRA STICKERS

EXTRA STICKERS

EXTRA STICKERS

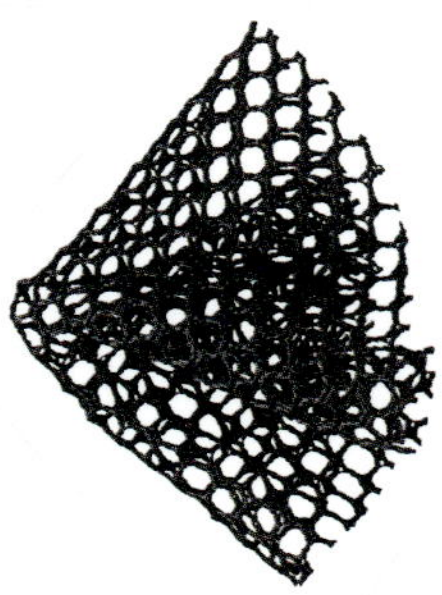

EXTRA STICKERS

EXTRA STICKERS

EXTRA STICKERS